Born of Common Hungers

Born of Common Hungers

Benedictine Women in Search of Connections

Photographs by ANNETTE BROPHY
Essays by MARA FAULKNER

Beauty of Catholic Life series

UNIVERSITY OF NOTRE DAME PRESS
NOTRE DAME AND LONDON

We gratefully acknowledge permission to reprint the following material:

"Alone" from *Oh Pray My Wings Are Gonna Fit Me Well* by Maya Angelou. Copyright © 1975 by Maya Angelou. Reprinted by permission of Random House, Inc.

From "Talk to me, Baby" by Michael Dennis Browne. Reprinted from Michael Dennis Browne: *The Sun Fetcher* by permission of Carnegie Mellon University Press, © 1978 by Michael Dennis Browne.

From "Making Peace" by Denise Levertov from *Breathing the Water*. Copyright © 1987 by Denise Levertov. Reprinted by permission of New Directions Publishing Corporation.

From "Life at War" by Denise Levertov from *The Sorrow Dance*. Copyright © 1966 by Denise Levertov. Reprinted by permission of New Directions Publishing Corporation.

"Pilgrim" taken from the English translation of *A Thousand Reasons for Living* by Dom Helder Câmara, published and copyright © 1987 by Darton, Longman and Todd Ltd, and used by permission of the publishers. In the United States and Canada, used by permission of Augsburg Fortress Publishers.

Library of Congress Cataloging-in-Publication Data

Brophy, Annette.
    Born of common hungers : Benedictine women in search of
connections / photographs by Annette Brophy ; essays by Mara Faulkner.
      p.   cm.
    ISBN 0-268-00703-9 (alk. paper).—ISBN 0-268-00704-7 (pbk. : alk paper)
    1. Benedictine nuns.   2. Benedictine monasteries.   3. Monastic and
religious life of women.   I. Faulkner, Mara.   II. Title.
BX4276.B76   1997
255′.97—dc21   97-22842
                                                           CIP

To Yvonne Sexton and to
Benedictine women around the world

Contents

Acknowledgments

The list of people who helped create this book and to whom we are grateful seems to grow every day. First, we thank Yvonne Sexton for believing in us when this book was only a dream. A generous grant from the Sexton Foundation made our travel and research possible. We thank our readers for encouragement and astute advice along the way—Sisters Anne Patrick, Nancy Hynes, Ephrem Hollermann, and Johanna Becker, and Fred and Rosemary Petters. We are indebted to Sister Delores Super, director of the Studium at St. Benedict's Monastery, for enthusiasm and financial support, and to the staff at the University of Notre Dame Press for their excitement about our book and their skill in editing and producing it.

The heart of this book is the six communities we profile. We are grateful for their hospitality and their willingness to have their stories told in words and pictures. We are especially grateful to our community, St. Benedict's Monastery, for protected work time.

Mara sends her thanks to her family and especially her sister, Judy Faulkner McGuire, whose love of rhythmical language and of Benedictine life made her an ideal reader. She also thanks the women she lives with and her students and colleagues at the College of St. Benedict, who have stood by her in good times and bad; her student workers—Anne Villendrer, Jodi Wallace, and Daniel Rosch—for typing endless drafts; Beverly Radaich for good cheer and computer wizardry; and the College of St. Benedict for a travel grant.

Annette thanks many people, especially her mom and dad, who always believed in her; Annette Jacobs and Joanne Dean, who listened endlessly to her dreams and whose sisterly loyalty and love sustained her through the making of this book; her brother Tim, whose quiet love and pride in the project were always there; Gretchen Berg, whose wisdom and enthusiasm cheered her on; and Galen Martini, who gave her a camera in the first place, encouraged her, trusted her, and inspired her to believe in her own vision.

This book belongs to these people and to many others. To all of you, blessings and thanks.

Photographer's Note

I call the camera my inner eye because it sees more than the eye sees—
something timeless, in its own space and rhythm. For the most part I've
stayed close to nature with my camera, close to silences, and close to
places of solitude. There are still places left in the world that hold stillnesses undisturbed. I like to go there as often as I can to find out what
the world is becoming. But at some point a small voice urged me away
from the security of the undisturbed stillnesses to something else that
was gnawing at my soul. I began to sense that the growing hunger within me was a keen desire for a broader look into monasteries other than
my own. I needed to find out firsthand what the world of Benedictine
monasticism is becoming. In particular, I wanted to hear the voices of
women telling the story of monasticism, historically and individually.

And so the concept was born and slowly began to take shape in my
mind. I wanted to photograph, in their own setting, Benedictine women
from all parts of the world. I needed a sensitive and gifted writer to col-
laborate with me in a search for profiles that would reveal the spirit and
the deeper pulse of the life force in each monastery we would visit. Mara,
with all her gifts and her interest in women's issues, was the perfect
choice.

In my years of photographing nature I reasoned that all things have
integrity; I have always respected that and have given myself permission
to spend a lot of time with my subject to ease into the relationship. I like
to create an antiphonal silence between myself and what I see, so that it
reveals something of the mystery and wholeness of its essence. But the
luxury of time was never given to me in our tour of the monasteries.
Schedules and availability ruled our limited time in each place. People,
unlike flowers, tend to pose or become self-conscious when confronted
with a camera unless they are distracted by a collaborator asking questions or gently urging them to tell their stories. And, yes, as we traveled
from monastery to monastery, it was the sisters telling us their stories
that seemed inevitably to allow the camera to catch them in their real
selves, brandishing the truth of what their lives are about, individually
and collectively.

Art is unpredictable. In the triangle of photographer, subject, and
viewer, it is, in the end, the viewer who will illuminate the images with
an emotional response to the truth, the stories, and the unanswered
questions raised here in this book.

Annette Brophy

Writer's Note

In writing about six Benedictine women's monasteries, including St. Benedict's Monastery, the one I belong to and know intimately, I tried to set aside the preconceptions formed over thirty years and see, feel, and hear freshly. I was guided by the women we talked with and by Annette's photographs, which often suggested a direction, a spirit, or a guiding metaphor, and nudged me away from using too many words. This experience reminded me again of Tillie Olsen's assertion that all writers have collaborators, those beings—often silent, often invisible—who make our work possible. I'd like to name a few of my collaborators, human and otherwise.

I became a writer partly because I grew up in the middle of North Dakota with its wheat fields, river bluffs, and endless skies. Summer days, smelling of alfalfa and clover, began with meadowlarks and ended after ten when the wide slow sunset faded. Winter days were brutally cold with shining, austerely carved drifts and an eloquent wind that howled at night around our house. What was a child to do with days and nights like those? Lucky enough to have no television and only the static of an old Philco radio, I filled the loneliness with books and music and stories I invented, sometimes dreaming alone in the abandoned chicken coop we called a play house and sometimes out loud with my brother and five sisters.

Almost as far back as I can remember, my father was blind. But he sang and danced and told such great stories that even thirty years after his death, I can hear the words and rhythms. In his early days he was an organizer for the Nonpartisan League, trying to get farmers to band together against the grain-buying conglomerates. I learned from Dennis Faulkner to revolt against injustice; and though he was a man of many opinions, firmly stated, he taught me to trust questions rather than ready answers.

My mother, Hattie Miller Faulkner, wasn't a reader, writer, or singer; in fact, she was one of the world's few true monotones. But this transplanted Minnesota woman made North Dakota flood silt sprout tomatoes as big as a plate and flowers so rare only she and Northrup King knew their names. Even though our house was tiny and stuffed with kids, flowers in jelly glasses stood in every room. She was a magician with a needle who turned feed sacks into first-day-of-school dresses, her stubby legs driving the treadle sewing machine far into the night, and her beautiful, strong hands turning rickrack and a bit of red thread into lace to edge the collar. When she died, she was knitting a pair of socks for some child with cold feet. Those socks were frugal rainbows made of many-colored yarn ends. She taught me to appreciate useful beauty and to create it, with words rather than yarn.

I came to St. Benedict's Monastery in 1964 already a writer and, in many ways, already a Benedictine. I came loving quiet and space and alert to the stories and bright visions behind ordinary faces and apparently humdrum lives. My parents taught us to question conventional standards of goodness, happiness, and beauty and to renounce rugged individualism in favor of responsibility for others. Every night, after praying for everyone in the family from grandma down to the cat, my mom had us ask God to bless "all the poor people." I don't know exactly who she had in mind, since we certainly fit into that category ourselves. Maybe she was asking us to trust in a God who loves the poor, however poverty is construed, and to stretch our hearts beyond the walls of our family, town, and country.

The members of my Benedictine community, the thousands of high school and college students I've taught, the peace movement and the women's movement, and the writers I love—chief among them Julian of Norwich and Tillie Olsen—have challenged and confirmed my early beliefs. Their mark is on this book.

Mara Faulkner

Born of Common Hungers

Introduction

Lying, thinking
Last night
How to find my soul a home
Where water is not thirsty
And bread loaf is not stone
I came up with one thing
And I don't believe I'm wrong
That nobody,
But nobody
Can make it here alone.

MAYA ANGELOU[1]

As Sister Annette Brophy and I visited six Benedictine women's monasteries in Germany, England, the United States, and Brazil, we asked the same question over and over: What values and beliefs guide your lives? In view of the great diversity that time, place, and circumstances have created among contemporary Benedictine communities, we wondered what the women in these communities have in common with each other, and, to stretch the question even further, what they have in common with the women and men who have lived Benedictine life for more than fifteen hundred years. From all this diversity, perhaps we would be able to distill the essence of the Benedictine spirit for ourselves, and then hand it on, bottled and corked, to our readers.

This question was genuine, but as places and faces impressed themselves on us, we began to see that the tenacious, knotty reality of these monasteries and the women who live in them would refuse to be boiled down into the blandness of formulas or generalities, religious or otherwise. Then another more troubling question superimposed itself on the original. We began to wonder what the Benedictine women Annette was photographing and I was interviewing have in common, not only with each other, but with the women outside their monasteries, the women with and for whom they work, the women whose faces appear on their television screens and in their newspapers.

The two women gazing from the facing page made this second question very concrete. They are Sister Aelrad Erwin, an English

Benedictine, and Dona Rosa, a Brazilian lay woman. Sister Aelrad, secure and sheltered in silence, offers warm hospitality to guests in Minster Abbey on the east coast of England. Dona Rosa supports herself and several grandchildren by keeping house for a priest who comes to Jussaral, her village in northeastern Brazil. She is also a midwife who has delivered hundreds of babies into certain poverty, malnutrition, and disease. These two hard-working women look surprisingly alike. When Sister Aelrad rolls up her sleeves to cook or clean, she takes off her religious veil and covers her hair with a simple scarf. Dona Rosa is also ready for work, an old shirt wrapped around her head. The likenesses between these two faces shocked us into asking what hungers, what riches, what poverties of body and spirit join and divide women like Sister Aelrad and Dona Rosa. What can they say to each other, learn from each other? Can Benedictine women dare to claim the common life, the common table with women who have little serenity or silence and who struggle daily to secure food for themselves and their children?

Why is it important to find commonalities between Benedictines and other women? Partly because monastic women are still trying to undo the damage of centuries when the Catholic church told us—and we sometimes believed—that we had chosen a higher and holier way of life than our married and single sisters. Even now, perhaps the fullness and the deprivations of our lives set an impassable barrier between us and other women. Yet, the call to community is central to Benedictine monasticism, extending far beyond the shelter of the monastery and challenging the members to great vulnerability and connectedness.

In a world fractured by every kind of division, the hunger for community is as strong outside monasteries as it is inside. But women of color like Audre Lorde and working women like Tillie Olsen have been asserting for many years that claims of sisterhood, brotherhood, or community lead only to the most specious unity without an awareness of the marks of history and circumstance on varied lives. In her famous essay "The Master's Tools Will Never Dismantle the Master's House," Lorde writes:

> As women, we have been taught either to ignore differences, or to view them as causes for separation and suspicion rather than as forces for change. Without community there is no liberation, only

the most vulnerable and temporary armistice between an individual and her oppression. But community must not mean a shedding of our differences, nor the pathetic pretense that these differences do not exist.[2]

Within Benedictine communities every woman calls every other woman *sister* and struggles to be free from the deceptively spacious prisons of class, status, and family. Yet it is easy for the communities themselves to remain trapped in those prisons, assuming that their lives are the norm and pushing women like Dona Rosa to the margins.

The photographs and essays in this book explore these overlapping questions by profiling six monasteries and a few of the women who are members of each one. Without presuming to make this a comprehensive study of a religious order that spans the globe, Annette and I chose communities linked by history to St. Benedict's Monastery in St. Joseph, Minnesota, where both of us have been members for many years. The first of these is St. Walburg Abbey in Eichstätt, Germany. This thousand-year-old abbey sent sisters to St. Marys, Pennsylvania, in 1852. Within five years of their arrival, the first small group of American Benedictines divided, some staying in St. Marys, some going to Erie, Pennsylvania, and another few making the long trip to St. Cloud, Minnesota, eventually settling eight miles west in St. Joseph.

Shortly before the outbreak of World War II, the abbey at Eichstätt again sent out pioneers, this time to Boulder, Colorado, and Minster, England, to establish places of refuge should Hitler make good his threat to occupy German monasteries. Though St. Walburg's survived the war intact, the sisters who had gone to Boulder and Minster chose to remain. Finally, in 1973, one sister from St. Benedict's Monastery in St. Joseph asked her community if she might go to Brazil. Within a few years, other sisters followed her, forming a small Benedictine community in the northeastern city of Recife. This recent foundation is not, properly speaking, a monastery or abbey, but simply a tiny community clinging to the edge of a Brazilian slum. It may survive and grow, or it may be gone within a few years. For now, the women there are doing what Benedictines have done throughout history—putting down tentative roots in a place that seems to need their presence.

Like all Benedictine women and men, these six communities live their lives under the guidance of the *Rule* written in the sixth century by Benedict of Nursia, the Italian founder of Benedictine monastic life. (Legend has it that his twin sister, Scholastica, founded the women's branch of Benedictinism at the same time. Though historians have found no solid evidence to support this story, Benedictine women continue to cherish it.) In spite of their common roots and *Rule,* these communities differ greatly in size, spirit, the work they do, and the ways in which they have blended Benedictine tradition with the needs and customs of the places where they settled.

The rich diversity we found made it seem even more important to tell these stories and show these pictures. Like the members of most religious communities, Benedictine women have been exalted, denigrated, parodied, and ignored, but rarely portrayed in their full humanness. Our years as members of a particular Benedictine monastery have taught Annette and me how hard it is to put this life into words or images. At its center is the single-hearted search for God, a search that is very quiet and ordinary, but also very strange and mysterious. It is tempting, therefore, to take refuge in silence, allowing the lives of Benedictines to speak to anyone who comes close enough to listen. But silence leaves an important story about women untold, a story of struggle, endurance, failure, and transcendence that might hearten other women and even reveal the voice of God speaking in history.

We have, therefore, based our exploration on some firm beliefs about women and their lives. First, we assume that Benedictines, like women throughout history, leave a trail of stories behind them and that those stories are interesting. This assumption counters many historical accounts in which Benedictine women are footnotes to the story of Benedictine men; it also counters the mass media's limited imagination of sisters' lives. For the media, these stories are apparently worth telling only when they can be made into jokes, when they overlap with a conventional romance plot, or when someone disguised as a sister brings the excitement of crime or underworld sleaze into the sisters' otherwise unstoried lives. It is true that the lives of Benedictines don't fit the pattern Western literary tradition has dictated for women: romance, leading either to happy or sacrificial marriage or to death. Recent stories about women's lives twist this familiar plot, adding sex, self-fulfillment, and the pursuit of wealth and power. But these stories too leave Benedictine women outside, to say nothing of most of the world's women.

Because we want to help broaden the circle of our shared imagination to include both Dona Rosa and Sister Aelrad, we join poet and essayist Adrienne Rich in "resisting amnesia." We agree with Rich that "we need to be looking above all for the greatness and variety of ordinary women, and how these women have collectively waged resistance. In searching that territory we find something better than individual heroines: the astonishing continuity of women's imagination of survival, persisting through the great and little deaths of daily life."[3] Rather than focusing on women within these six communities who are nationally or internationally known as scholars and religious leaders, we photographed and interviewed sisters whose lively faces and words would be found only in monastery archives.

We have set these women's lives within the context of their monasteries. We don't see the women as exceptions whose courage and steadfastness happened in isolation; rather, we think that their communities helped set into flight their gifts of mind, heart, and hand. Because the interplay of temporal and material circumstances has shaped each of these monasteries, we have lightly sketched their histories. Each of them has a particular spirit, a particular way of refracting Benedictine monasticism. Another pair of observers, with a different writer's and photographer's eyes, would no doubt characterize each community differently; and the members themselves might be surprised to see how they appear to a pair of outsiders.

Rather than a bottle for preserving Benedictinism, we want these pictures and words to be fertile ground where women and men, whether Benedictine or not, can plant their feet. And rather than imposing links where they may not exist, we show what we found and leave it to our observers and readers to discover bridges and barriers, offer challenges, and forge alliances born of common hungers.

Whom we feed, sustain us.
Who need us, we keep breathing for.

MICHAEL DENNIS BROWNE[4]

St. Walburg Abbey

EICHSTÄTT, GERMANY

At first, St. Walburg Abbey in Eichstätt, Germany, seems like a museum, and the sisters like curators of old paintings and old ways. Benedictine women have lived at St. Walburg's since the abbey's founding in 1035. The red-roofed baroque buildings standing in the hills near Eichstätt date mainly from the seventeenth and eighteenth centuries. Large, dark paintings and statues, some of them more than five hundred years old, line the abbey's dim halls. The sisters are guardians of the tomb of St. Walburga, the Anglo-Saxon woman who came to southern Germany in the eighth century. Every year hundreds of people come to her tomb to pray for healing or to offer thanks.

The seventy or so sisters who now make up this community wear the traditional Benedictine habit, which looks very much like the clothing worn by St. Walburga on fifteenth-century tapestries and paintings. They live and work within the confines of the abbey, leaving only rarely for vacations, education, or health care.

But spend a few days in this abbey in the company of these busy, intelligent, humorous women and you will find that this community is less a museum than a rich garden or field that skillful, patient farmers have tended for nine hundred years; tended so well, in fact, that it is more fertile now than it was when they turned over the first shovelful of earth. Like all good farmers, the sisters don't waste anything. They save whatever is in danger of being discarded by a throw-away society, storing it until it becomes the soil out of which new life grows.

The sisters are conservationists who use things responsibly, "so we can answer for them," as Sister Fides Nossek puts it. The seventy-four of them have one car and one driver; they conserve fuel and water and don't use toxic chemicals in cleaning or gardening. Even without chemicals, they raise all their own vegetables in bountiful wide-rowed plots, and flowers bloom everywhere. In June, pansies, tulips, and bridal wreath border the paths winding into the hills behind the abbey.

Because the sisters support themselves, they recycle the many donations that come to them, sending money and hundreds of parcels of food every year to needy people around the world. And because they don't readily tear down old buildings, the gates, the doors, the very architecture of the abbey preserve the Eichstätt community's history. Memories of justice and injustice, courage and adventure are alive and instructive in those buildings.

Determined to secularize Europe, in 1806 Napoleon seized all the churches and monasteries in what is now Germany. He gave St. Walburg's property, buildings, and assets to Bavarian princes who had supported him in his wars. The government sent all the young sisters home, allowing only the abbess and the twenty-four older sisters to stay in the abbey. Thirteen of them survived the thirty years of secularization. In 1835 King Ludwig I of Bavaria restored the abbey to the Benedictine sisters and allowed them to begin receiving new members. The restoration was only partial. Since 1806, the state has owned all the property, buildings, and art pieces; the sisters live there and maintain the place, with some help from various historical societies.

The monastery library traces the effects of war and poverty on St. Walburg Abbey. Like most Benedictine monasteries down through history, St. Walburg's has always treasured learning. The Old Book Library holds over five thousand books, the oldest dating back to the fifteenth century. One of the most precious is an antiphonary, an illuminated prayerbook Sister Susanna Jennigen copied and illuminated three hundred years ago. It is very large—two feet by three feet—so that twenty-four sisters could read from it during the Divine Office. Though they were often hungry and cold during the period of secularization, the sisters safeguarded the old books, including this antiphonary. As Sister Mechtildis Denz says, "The sisters folded their arms over it and preferred to freeze rather than burn it as fuel in the furnace."

From 1914 until very recently, St. Walburg's, like the rest of Germany, paid the high price of two world wars. During those decades the community was too poor to afford books, so there are large gaps in the collection. Only within the past few years have they been able to enlarge the library and buy books again.

The Church of St. Walburga, which the abbey shares with the surrounding parish, holds another memory too valuable to discard—the memory of class divisions within the monastic community. For hundreds of years, women entered the community as choir sisters or lay sisters. Choir sisters, from well-to-do or aristocratic families, traditionally were the community artists, scholars, and leaders. Lay sisters often came to St. Walburg's from nearby farms and continued the work they had done at home—cooking, cleaning, gardening, farming. Choir sisters sang the whole Divine Office in Latin; lay sisters prayed the rosary in their native German. Lay sisters couldn't vote on community decisions. In the church, the lay sisters sat on little wooden seats physically separated both from the other sisters and from the parishioners.

These class divisions reflected those in the surrounding society but ignored the admonitions in the Gospels and the *Rule* of St. Benedict that erase distinctions between rich and poor, and between free-born people and slaves. The divisions have gradually disappeared at St. Walburg's. In the newest community constitution, approved in 1988, no practical distinctions at all exist between lay and choir sisters, and, in fact, the community has abandoned these titles.

It would be easy enough for the St. Walburg community to root out these memories and turn their backs on those rough wooden chairs. Instead, when the sisters take visitors on tour, they point them out and explain their place in history. Maybe they are a concrete reminder to the community to be alert to great injustices so deeply embedded in society and psyche that they are literally invisible.

The sisters at Eichstätt rarely look away from the injustices and suffering surrounding them. They read a daily newspaper and listen to world news every day at breakfast, a variation on the traditional table reading. Sister Fides says, "The Gulf War was a terrible time for us." Even if they didn't look for it, suffering would find them. Every day, in dozens of "bidding letters," people from all over the world pour out their stories of grief and tragedy.

The sisters' response is the same as it has been for over nine hundred years. Six times a day, every day, they bring to common prayer the broken bits of life the day has given to them. They take all of it—their own exhaustion or loneliness, the world's wars and starvation, the sickness and despair of the letter writers—and turn it into song. For nine hundred years, people with and without faith in God have counted on the sisters to take in their arms the inconsolable sufferings of the world. Patient faith in the transforming power of prayer is the great sun that warms this place and radiates from it.

The same gate still stands in the abbey courtyard through which sisters left St. Walburg's to go to the United States and England. In 1852, less than twenty years after the government restored the abbey to the sisters, a German Benedictine monk named Boniface Wimmer knocked on the door. He asked Abbess Edwarda Schnitzer for sisters to teach the growing number of German settlers in the United States. He had already established a men's monastery in Latrobe, Pennsylvania, from which monks went to St. Marys.

This small, poor settlement, still surrounded by virgin forest, became the birthplace of the women's Benedictine order in the United States. With only forty-two members, St. Walburg's was struggling for stability; yet, from 1852 to 1855 they sent twelve sisters to Pennsylvania, most of them women in their twenties and thirties. The move demanded faith, courage, and daring on the part of the sisters who left. (Benedicta Riepp, the leader of the first group, was only twenty-seven when she and her companions sailed for America.)

What must this exodus have meant to the sisters who stayed behind, waving good-bye? Did they remind each other of the dear old story of how Walburga, Leoba, and many other young Benedictine sisters came from England to southern Germany in the eighth century, when Germany was virgin forest? Did they have an intuition that they were saying good-bye forever, and that their sisters, planted in Pennsylvania soil, would soon undergo the mutations necessary to survive in a vastly different cultural and religious climate from the one they were leaving behind? Did they freely scatter this seed, certain that life fully given always continues?

SISTER MECHTILDIS DENZ

Sister Mechtildis Denz knows that monastic life offers no guarantees. She says:

> To live in an enclosed convent you have to be a big person. Otherwise you spend all your time circling around yourself, finding little ailments and petty grievances and obeying little rules.
>
> Or you can be middle-sized, an ordinary citizen looking after your own comfort, interested in a little bit of the world, a little bit of suffering. That's an easy life.
>
> To live a big life is very hard because your skin becomes thinner. You feel more what's right and not right in your own abbey. Is it really a life for God? Our job is to heal here, then to take that healing to all the people who come to us.

Sister Mechtildis is lured away from pettiness or easy comfort by the children she teaches. With her sensitive face and agile scholar's mind, she is nothing like the hard-boiled, ruler-swinging grade-school teachers of United State's Catholic folklore. She repeats an old German saying that translates, "The children are close to our skin." What she means is that she feels the troubles of the young people she teaches as if they were her own. Because she has learned to read the marks of divorce, poverty, neglect, and abuse on her students' bodies and spirits, she also knows the injustices and brokenness of her society. She brings them all to the sheltering, healing arms of the community.

In 1835, when King Ludwig restored St. Walburg Abbey, he told the impoverished sisters that they had to find a way to support themselves. Legend says that they had three choices—brew beer, sell St. Walburga's healing oil, or staff a day school for girls run by the government. They chose teaching, and for the first time in eight hundred years began a work that took them outside the monastery. They have been teaching ever since in the government school adjoining their property. Mother Franziska Kloos, the current abbess, was a master teacher before she became abbess, and education is close to her heart. Under her leadership, the community recently built a bright, airy kindergarten for seventy-five children.

Besides teaching, Mechtildis also serves as the abbey librarian, using a computer to catalog five-hundred-year-old books. She loves the old books and the clues they hold to a history that has still to be written. Mechtildis wants to explore in this library an idea that scholars like Gerda Lerner affirm—that St. Walburg Abbey, like many religious communities, has always been a place where women's minds could range with some degree of freedom. Even in centuries when most girls and women were illiterate or, at best, trained to be docile and decorative, the choir sisters at Eichstätt were studying theology and mysticism.

On the flyleaves of thirty-five books, Mechtildis has found the name of Amanda Frumin and the date when she received each one. This precious cluster of books gave Sister Mechtildis the idea for an intriguing piece of scholarship. If she were to read these books in the same order as Amanda Frumin did, what would she discover about the education and spiritual development of an eighteenth-century woman? What books did family members or spiritual directors consider appropriate at different stages of her life? What were her contemporaries in and out of the abbey reading? Mechtildis holds these books reverently, as if their substance and the marks of earlier hands communicate energy and wisdom across the centuries.

SISTER WALBURGA GRETSCHMANN

In the cold, quiet *weberei*, or weaver's room, sisters still practice the ancient art of tapestry making. At Eichstätt this art is not learned primarily from books. One generation passes it into the hands of the next generation, and the work of earlier weavers offers inspiration, filling the room with subtle color.

Today, Sister Walburga Gretschmann is weaving a design called the Burning Bush. The warp, or lengthwise yarn, is plain, sturdy, undyed wool, but the woof of silk is so bright it seems to set the wool on fire. Under Sister Walburga's hands, yellow, orange, deep rose, and red flicker and blaze on an ocean-blue background. She learned her craft from Sister Deocara, who died in 1967. Now Sister Walburga is teaching it to her apprentice, Sister Maria Magdelena Zunker.

SISTER MARIA MAGDELENA ZUNKER

Sister Maria Magdelena came to St. Walburg's in 1987 from a life of travel and scholarship. She earned a doctorate in archeology before becoming a Catholic and a Benedictine.

Maria Magdelena says that weaving is a good work for a contemplative because "the spirit of God and of Benedictine life is in it, and I can communicate that spirit to the people who buy my work." Her work belies the serenity and calm of the *weberei*. One of her designs is the Leviathan of Psalm 104, a sea creature God created as a playmate, or so the psalm says. The Leviathan that emerged on Maria Magdelena's loom is a fierce and fanciful beast, part dolphin, part Loch Ness monster, with many feet and a dragon's head. She created this design, Maria Magdelena says, as an image of herself, God's playful friend, swimming in the deep waters of a life devoted wholly to God.

I am a frayed and nibbled survivor in a fallen world, and I am getting along. I am aging and eaten and have done my share of eating too. I am not washed and beautiful, in control of a shining world in which everything fits, but instead am wandering awed about on a splintered wreck I've come to care for, whose gnawed trees breathe a delicate air, whose bloodied and scarred creatures are my dearest companions, and whose beauty beats and shines not in its imperfections but overwhelmingly in spite of them, under the wind-rent clouds, upstream and down. Simone Weil says simply, "Let us love the country of here below. It is real; it offers resistance to love."

ANNIE DILLARD[5]

Mount St. Benedict Monastery

ERIE, PENNSYLVANIA

To keep them sure-footed on the turning earth, communities, like individuals, need gravity, a force strong enough to balance the thrill of weightlessness, dispersion, and novelty. The call at the heart of Benedictinism "to earnestly seek God" would seem to be an unshakable center of gravity. The *Rule* of Benedict even offers advice on where to look for God: in the poor and the sick, in guests and pilgrims, in the old and the young, in community members and leaders. The *Rule* says, "Never turn away when someone needs your love."[6] The sisters of Mount St. Benedict Monastery in Erie, Pennsylvania, like generous people in every age and place, ask themselves who needs their love and what concrete forms that love should take.

In the beginning, the answer was evident. In 1856, when the sisters from Eichstätt were barely settled in St. Marys, Pennsylvania, four women left for Erie to open a grade school. Because recent German and Irish immigrants, most of them poor, needed education and health care, that's what the sisters provided. For the next hundred years, they taught, nursed, and administered schools, colleges, hospitals, and retirement homes.

In the 1970s, as more and more Catholic schools closed and religious orders gave up their ownership of big institutions, the Erie community saw that they needed a new center of gravity to hold them together as they moved into many different kinds of work and to keep them moving "in a gospel direction," as one member says. Under the leadership of Sister Joan Chittister and several other far-seeing women, the community chose not a new kind of work but a specific commitment to social justice.

In 1978, the community voted to join the movement for nuclear disarmament. This press release made their commitment public and immediate:

> The Benedictine sisters of Erie will stand in a corporate way for the nuclear disarmament of the nations in behalf of the value of created life. . . . Each of us individually will stand for that purpose in whatever way we can wherever we are.[7]

The community promised financial support for various peace groups, and each sister wrote and signed a description of how she would help carry out this commitment to nonviolence. Every four years, the sisters reexamine both the substance of their commitment and their faithfulness to it. Even in the post–Cold War years, they have held steady in their opposition to nuclear weapons and have added a promise to explore and expose the links between militarism and the oppression of women.

Considering the scope of these issues, the community could have taken shelter in abstractions or utopian dreams. Instead, standing together and speaking publicly has made this community energetic, creative, and practical. As the community philosophy says, "We accept the challenge to shape the future of the human community and respond with courage, knowing that with God all things are possible."

The phrase *down-to-earth* takes on a whole new meaning when you apply it to the Erie community. These women are planted on the earth and, more firmly still, among the people of Erie. In the late 1960s one wing of their mother-house in Erie was condemned. Instead of rebuilding in the city, they moved onto a hundred acres on the shore of Lake Erie. The community bought this piece of property over sixty years ago and have run a summer camp for children there ever since. This haven on the lake's rocky shore is graced by a spacious monastery, gardens and greenhouses, and hermitages standing among birch trees.

The community reaches out from their haven and welcomes people in. Guests and retreatants are plentiful at liturgies and meals; and until recently, one of the sisters was a registered foster care provider, giving a good start in life to a procession of babies.

Many of the sisters never left the city, and in the past thirty years the community has reclaimed a square block near downtown Erie that would almost surely have surrendered to inner-city decay without their steady presence. This block and the monastery are only seven miles apart, separated by a General Electric plant that provides erratic employment and, closer to the city, run-down and often deserted buildings. On one of them graffiti condemns BLUE-EYED DEVILS. In the summer, a heavy, rotten smell hangs over the city.

But the square block the sisters have reclaimed is beautiful. The buildings are old but well-kept, and in the summer Headstart kids plant garden plots. Because this block is the site of their old motherhouse, the sisters already owned some of the buildings and property; but they went into debt to buy and remodel almost all the other buildings on the block. Two of them are houses where groups of sisters live because they think real presence demands more than coming to the city to work, and retreating to the country in the evening.

What happens on that square block and in the other places the sisters work? It's tempting to say *everything,* but that answer isn't quite accurate. These women seem to leave well-worn paths and gravitate toward the margins where undone work and forgotten people linger. They lead the way and invite others to join them.

Juan

A good example is the Erie Second Harvest Foodbank. Fifteen years ago the city asked the Benedictines to sponsor and administer the struggling Erie Community Foodbank whose assets were a hundred dollars, a little food, and a few interested workers. In 1992, after ten years of Sister Augusta Hamel's leadership, the Bank had supplied five and a half million pounds of food to over three hundred soup kitchens, pantries, and emergency shelters. In one year these agencies fed sixty thousand people in Erie and the surrounding area. Here, as in many middle-sized cities surrounded by farms, hunger is invisible and easy to ignore. Suspecting that the need was greater than even she knew, Sister Augusta got a community foundation to study hunger in the area. She immediately communicated their dismal findings to religious and civic groups. She says, "People were outraged by what was right here in our own community. As a result, they came together and supported our efforts to alleviate hunger." In 1993, when the Benedictines were sure of stable civic support for the Foodbank, they returned sponsorship to the city and Sister Augusta moved on to the Chicago area Second Harvest Foodbank.[8]

But these women know that feeding sixty thousand hungry people in Erie, Pennsylvania, a city surrounded by rich farmland, is cause for anger rather than rejoicing. They turn their anger into work for broad social change and into programs to help people lift themselves out of poverty and despair. On that same city block they administer St. Mary's grade school for inner-city children and bilingual Headstart and day-care programs for the children of migrant workers.

The St. Benedict Education Center offers high school equivalency and job training programs to single parents so they can get off welfare. The students are primarily women, of course, but single men are also welcome. Ten or so sisters provide this education in one of the newly renovated buildings on that amazing block. The building was St. Benedict's Academy, a girls' high school the Erie sisters ran for decades. Though a security system guards the outside doors, the renovation opened up the inside to gracious, welcoming stairways, curved arches, and high-ceilinged rooms. Light pours in, touching the paintings and photographs on the walls. On the third floor is Still-point, a prayer room to which Sister Jean Lavin invites the people in the job training programs. Sister Jean says:

> Some have never experienced five minutes alone and don't have any idea who they really are. The gift of self is the best gift possible. . . . Many of the women have been beaten down and abused most of their lives, and they think they're worthless.
>
> In class I try to teach basic life skills and build up their self-confidence. If they choose to come to Still-point, I try to teach them to pray so that they know God loves them right now, just as they are.[9]

The sisters at Mount St. Benedict Monastery speak off-handedly about these and a half-dozen other programs they've dreamed up and established in Erie and all around the world. They always keep their projects in the public eye so that others can join them in their work, but if visitors seem too impressed with their accomplishments, they quickly disclaim perfection or superwoman status by pointing out the problems they face. They are a small community with big debts; some wonder who will support them when they're old. Others dislike the steady flow of guests. Some worry about the risks the community has taken in providing sanctuary for Central American refugees, while others would like to be even more radical in countering sexism and violence in church and society.

Yet, convinced that the world is one world, they readily and lightly step out of security and stagnation, guided only by the earth's curve underfoot. The explanations they offer are simple but worth pondering: "We've had good leaders who spread knowledge, responsibility, and authority throughout the community"; "We risk being eccentric, out-of-step"; and the most steadying of all, "We're a faith-filled community."

SISTER MARLENE BERTKE

The day we first met her, Sister Marlene Bertke was packed and ready to fly to Mexico. She was to join a delegation of United States citizens escorting Guatemalan refugees back to their home country. During Guatemala's many years of civil unrest and government violence, at least forty thousand people fled to refugee camps in Mexico. Most of them are Mayan Indians whose lands were seized and villages wiped out by government troops. The refugees themselves and human rights groups in Guatemala had negotiated with the government for their return and resettlement. Marlene was radiant with happiness that she was helping escort them home and that her sisters were sending her on her way.

The next day, when the president of Guatemala dissolved the legislature and the delegation postponed the trip, Marlene wept, "I feel as if I'm nine months pregnant and can't deliver this baby."

Marlene's desire to work for economic and political justice in Central America had begun much more than nine months earlier. In the 1960s, as a member of St. Walburga's Benedictine Monastery in Covington, Kentucky, Marlene was head of the girls' high school her community sponsored. Like many Catholic boarding schools, this one attracted the daughters of wealthy Central American families. Marlene tried to talk with the girls about inequalities in their home countries, but, as she says, they couldn't see injustice but only the charity their families offered: "We give them food, clothes, a first-day-of-school dress," the girls told her.

By this time violence in El Salvador was escalating, and Marlene knew she had to do more than talk to teenage girls. She joined the Pax Center in Erie, a group of sisters and lay men and women who came together in the early 1970s to study and work for peace. Originally, Marlene planned to return to Covington and start a center modeled after Erie's. But she realized that in her community she was "*the* voice speaking for peace and justice."

While she loves the Covington community and respects their choices, Marlene transferred to Mount St. Benedict in the early 1980s. "I want to be part of a community that speaks together," she says, "a small part of a prophetic community rather than a lone prophet's voice."

It's easy to see that commitment to dispossessed people in Central America has a firm foothold at Mount St. Benedict; it is not simply Marlene's pet project. About twelve years ago, in spite of fears that their leaders would be jailed and their property confiscated, the Benedictine community voted to become a sanctuary for Central American political refugees. Since then several sisters have helped resettle refugees in Erie and Canada and have visited camps in Mexico and Mayan villages in Guatemala. They came back to the community with stories of anguish and hope and concrete plans to lobby the United States and Guatemalan governments to end military terrorism.

Three times a day the sisters come together to pray, inviting neighbors and guests to join them. While their prayer is the Divine Office, the traditional prayer of Benedictines around the world, they always shape it to fit the life of the community and of the world. The day Marlene was supposed to leave for Mexico, the prioress, Sister Phyllis Schleicher, was ready to offer the community's blessing on her and her group. When the plans changed, so did the community's prayer. It became a plea for the struggling Guatemalan people and a hopeful look forward to the day when Marlene would be called again.

SISTER CAROLYN GORNY-KOPKOWSKI

The women at Mount St. Benedict Monastery struggle with the weight of their possessions. What does it mean to speak with and for the dispossessed in Erie, the United States, and around the world when your community owns a hundred beautiful acres touching Lake Erie? Their debts and mortgages are real but invisible and mute; the buildings and land are only too visible and speak eloquently of wealth, security, and power.

Sister Carolyn Gorny-Kopkowski, the administrator of Glinodo retreat and conference center, is especially alert to this problem of possessions. Before she came to Glinodo, Carolyn coordinated the Emmaus soup kitchen in Erie. There she saw desperate inequalities firsthand as she helped provide food, a friendly word, and a listening ear to a daily stream of hungry and homeless people. The food they served was often Second Harvest food—the gleanings from supermarkets, restaurants, and wedding dinners. "Unless you're deaf and blind," Carolyn says, "it has to affect you."

At Emmaus and now at Glinodo, Carolyn tries to "listen to my own body, listen to the corporate body, listen to this land and the lake and the trees." Her listening has told her that the "corporate body" is almost as hungry for quiet places and earth underfoot as for food. So, Carolyn, her community, and their friends are working to make Glinodo accessible to as many people as possible, those who can afford it and those who can't, those who can walk the trail and climb the rocks and those in wheelchairs and on crutches. Thanks to donated money and labor, many groups come free, and wheelchair ramps slant gently from the cabins down to the lake.

Listening to their hundred acres with its lake and trees has convinced Carolyn and her community to hold it lightly but protectively, balancing people's need for green space with the land's need for protection from pollution and exploitation. With their talent for turning ideals into concrete action, the sisters welcome many groups to Glinodo every year for environmental study, much of it funded by grants. And every time they publish their community newsletter, they plant another tree.

This beloved soul was preciously knitted to God in its making, by a knot so subtle and so mighty that it is united in God. In this uniting it is made endlessly holy. Furthermore, God wants us to know that all the souls that will be saved in heaven without end are knit in this knot, and united in this union, and made holy in this holiness.

DAME JULIAN OF NORWICH[10]

St. Benedict's Monastery

ST. JOSEPH, MINNESOTA

The *Rule* of St. Benedict is filled with homely metaphors. The monastery is "the school for the service of the Lord" where all are learners whose eyes kindle at ideas, questions, and beauty. In this school, everything from the psalms, to a guest at the door, to work in the kitchen teaches about God. The *Rule* admonishes community members to treat kettles and dishes, hoes and spades, pens and paint brushes—all the monastery's tools—as reverently as they treat the altar vessels. The leader of the monastery must also be gentle in correcting faults; "otherwise, by rubbing too hard to remove the rust, she may break the vessel." The monastery is a workshop where women and men practice "the spiritual craft," using such tools as silence, generosity, hospitality, and peacemaking. St. Benedict calls the daily praying of the Divine Office the *opus Dei,* the *work of God.* This metaphor asserts that prayer is the central task of the monastery and that work of all kinds has something in common with prayer. Like prayer, work serves God, is the way to God; both are necessary, regular, leisurely, full of wonder; both deserve to be done mindfully, beautifully. Both sing a song of praise.

Taken together, these metaphors of school and workshop knit monastic life into a sturdy, seamless fabric, transforming all the events of every day into the work of God and promising an inner simplicity that does not easily unravel.

But the 140-year history of St. Benedict's Monastery in St. Joseph, Minnesota, shows that this seamlessness is easier to achieve in the momentary balance of language than in the lives of Benedictine communities and their members.

In the light-filled gathering place adjoining the chapel at St. Benedict's stand two limestone carvings created by Joseph O'Connell.

In the first carving, a Benedictine woman buffeted by storms holds a schoolchild in sheltering arms. The sculpture calls to mind the sudden, deadly blizzards that roar across midwestern prairies, the early hostility the founders of this community faced from many quarters, and the cultural realities that sometimes threaten to sweep the community off its moorings.

The second carving seems to grow out of the very earth from which the stone was quarried. No storms can shake that grounded woman.

These two carvings portray in stone the two insepara-ble calls of Benedictine life which the *Rule* expresses in metaphor—to pray and to serve. Shaped like every human community by the culture in which it finds itself, St. Benedict's Monastery tries to hold these two calls in balance.

In 1857, seven women came to St. Cloud, Minnesota, from Pennsylvania. Six years later they moved to nearby St. Joseph. At first, the sisters supported themselves by giving music and needlework lessons to the children of Protestant merchants, generally more prosperous than the German Catholic farmers who regularly faced drought and grasshopper infestations. The sisters also did laundry for Benedictine monks and, in truly desperate times, went begging from farm to farm.

The women suffered cold, hunger, and disease along with the people they were serving. Ornate iron crosses in the cemetery at St. Joseph tell of sisters dying at age thirty or twenty-one or nineteen. Mother Benedicta Riepp, the brave young woman who led the first group of sisters from Germany to the United States, died here at age thirty-six, probably of tuberculosis.

Soon requests for the sisters' services as teachers and nurses came from all over. Within twenty-five years of their arrival in St. Joseph, this community staffed twenty-eight grade schools, three hospitals, three boarding schools for Ojibwe Indian children, and three orphanages. In 1925 the community borrowed the then astounding sum of two million dollars to build a large modern hospital in St. Cloud. They could not know that the Great Depression was on the horizon and that many of their patients in the next decade would not be able to pay for their care. It took years of frugality and hard work—sometimes around the clock—to pay off that debt.

A girls' finishing school and academy, opened in 1880, grew into a high school and, in 1913, into the College of St. Benedict. It was fully accredited as a liberal arts college in 1933, and now, in partnership with St. John's University, enrolls thirty-five hundred students.

These kinds of work necessitated many modifications in the way of life the sisters had brought with them from Germany. Some of them worried that they were losing the essential balance the *Rule* promises; but to their credit they never gave up the work of God, the communal praying of the Divine Office. In 1881, they began praying a shortened form; their return to the full office in 1929 was a cause for rejoicing.

In spite of poverty, hostility, and hard work, St. Benedict's community grew fast. Many young women came and stayed, so that within twenty-five years, the community expanded from six to 164 members. History suggests several social and economic reasons for this swift growth. But deeper reasons lie not in history but in the mystery of the human heart, hungering in every age for a simple life where the search for God is primary.

The community continued to grow for a hundred years, with thirty or more young women joining every year. At one point St. Benedict's had over a thousand members. Since the 1960s, interrelated developments in church and society led many women to leave the community and far fewer to join. Yet, even with all this attrition and the formation of eleven new communities, ten of which have become independent monasteries, St. Benedict's still has about 430 members—an oddity among Benedictine monasteries, which typically number from twelve to a hundred.

Even a cursory reading of the community's history makes it seem larger still, revealing an astonishing variety of people and cultures knitted into the knot of its life. As women went out in groups or singly—to Utah, Puerto Rico, China, Japan, the Bahamas, Brazil—they asked the heart of the community to expand to accommodate the worlds and peoples they met, a meeting that was often unsettling, even painful, but always enriching.

The archives hold letters and memoirs from the six sisters who went to Peking, China, in 1930 to establish a women's college. (These six considered themselves lucky to be chosen from among two hundred volunteers.) Sister Ronayne Gergen, who taught in China and Taiwan until her death there in 1991, writes in her memoirs of the Japanese invasion of China in 1935. At first, the sisters helped nurse wounded Chinese soldiers. "I'll never forget the anguish of those days," she writes, "and the terribly wounded young soldiers, most of them farm boys. . . ." The sisters spent the war years under house arrest or in refugee or concentration camps, sharing the terror and privations of their fellow Chinese prisoners but also setting up makeshift schools.[11]

These images and stories belong to all the women at St. Benedict's. Their memories also hold thousands of students taught in grade schools, high schools, and colleges, babies brought into the world by labor-room nurses, eyes closed in death by hospice nurses and families comforted by chaplains, aching bodies soothed by massaging hands and spirits soothed by gentle listening.

The history and the present reality of St. Benedict's Monastery show that the ears of these women are attuned to sounds of need, and they, like all generous people, want to respond. Perhaps because of the community's size and complexity and the range and intensity of its work, the early misgivings about balance and integrity keep coming back. Without quiet time to listen, to pay attention, to question, will the best-intentioned work be thoughtless, even violent? Good work—scholarship, teaching, gardening, cooking, ceramics—heals both the worker and the work and does not destroy the interwoven human and natural ecology. But the community's life is entwined with many other institutions, from the Catholic church to the United States health care system to the government of Brazil, each with its own demands and its inexorable pull to stasis. The integrity of the community's work demands a replenishing solitude to help decide what to take over the doorstep and what to leave outside.

Even more important, with ever-increasing demands on their time and attention, where will these women find the quiet space and time essential for the work of seeking God to which they gave their lives?

In her essay, "Why Monastic Life in the Late Twentieth Century: Testimonies of Perception," Sister Katherine Kraft traces the dream and the reality of her thirty-eight years as a member of this monastery, living a life she loves passionately but which, for her, seems threatened:

> There it was, my dream: to be ensnared by the love of God; prayer as the best deal around; the life of the gaze—that's what I think I was after. Painfully, my life . . . has lost its romance. If the word "romance" puts you off, substitute enthusiasm, energy, zest or zeal. I find myself unable to dismiss it all lightly as merely the expected loss of one's youthful idealism. Rather, it seems intimately connected with insufficient nourishment, a famine of my heart and spirit. . . . There has to be time to feed the spirit, to refresh the soul, to ponder the Word of Life. My heart says, "I've got to do something about that before I die."[12]

Sister Katherine describes eloquently the challenge her community has faced throughout its history. But this "famine of the heart and spirit" gnaws at many people in technological societies; and as history and literature show, women have often felt its pain. One literary depiction is Tillie Olsen's famous story "I Stand Here Ironing," in which an anonymous mother ponders her life. She raised her children through Depression and war, first as a single mother and then as a working mother who had to help support them. As she tries to understand her oldest daughter, she wonders when she will have time "to remember, to sift, to weigh, to estimate, to total? I will start and there will be an interruption and I will have to gather it all together again." A mother's ear, she says, is not her own but "must always be wracked and listening for the child cry, the child call."[13]

The "life of the gaze" Sister Katherine longs for is not an escape from messy, inconvenient human life. Contemplative prayer always leads to the inner wilderness where God and the self are knit together with "all that is," as Dame Julian of Norwich says.[14] In that wilderness there is no turning away from the child cry, the concentration camp, the violent streets.

The women who make up St. Benedict's Monastery love and honor their history and the women who set out with faith and sheer nerve on trails no one had blazed for them. The community may now take a new, perhaps equally courageous direction called for by a world still hungry for food, shelter, and creative work, but also for a spirituality as grounded as Joseph O'Connell's praying woman.

That new direction may already be present in hints, faintly traced clues, and barely audible voices.

SISTER NANCY BAUER

With a photographer's eye for the particular and a journalist's passion for the concrete, Sister Nancy Bauer turns abstractions into flesh and blood. She also asks questions that challenge whatever appears natural or inevitable.

After Catholic grade school and high school, Nancy stopped going to church. "After a long time of silence," she says, she started praying again when her niece, Joy, needed surgery right after birth. "Of course, when you pray for someone else, something happens to you," Nancy says.

Nancy came to St. Benedict's Monastery in 1976 with a degree in photojournalism from the University of Minnesota. Soon after, she took a part-time job as a reporter for the St. Cloud *Visitor,* a diocesan paper founded in 1938 with a circulation of over forty thousand. In 1990, she became editor, the first woman in the paper's history to hold this position. In 1992 and 1994, the *Visitor* won first place for general excellence from the National Catholic Press Association. Nancy herself has written award-winning editorials and produced award-winning photoessays bringing the worlds of Jamaica, El Salvador, and Venezuela to her Minnesota readers.

Nancy acknowledges that her job as editor has brought her recognition both outside and inside her religious community. She says, "A lot of my acceptance in the community happened because of professional success. When I started writing editorials, people began to realize I had a voice and something to say." She also realizes that stating her views on divisive issues, visiting developing countries, and even tracking down an elusive detail at midnight, a few hours before deadline, are part of her search for God, "her deepest-down value." As she says, "I needed to learn that seeking God happens in the rush and panic and pressure of being editor of the *Visitor*" as well as in long, quiet days spent in the woods, with only her silent camera for company.

In the next breath Nancy asks one of her unsettling questions: "What is my 'wonderful job' at the *Visitor* doing to me and to my community?" She adds, "If I thought through my real views of monastic life, I probably wouldn't have the job I do," a job that keeps her running, literally, around the world and often draws her away from the regularity of community life. She wonders aloud how many lives she can live and how much diversity her community can accommodate before the fabric begins to fray.

Taking a historian's long view, Nancy considers it "an honor and a privilege to be part of something bigger than this generation and century." She calls the women who have been members of St. Benedict's for fifty or seventy-five years her "saving grace." She wonders, though, how her generation will ever gain the depth she sees in them in a community that is always in transition and a world that does not prize lifelong commitment.

When she came to this community, Nancy was determined to "see everything new." Now, after twenty years, she would like to do that again, through the medium of words that name concrete situations and do not take refuge in bland religious rhetoric. "Let's have a free-for-all," she says.

Nancy senses in herself and in her community "something scarier than fear but not to the point of despair." The fear is not just personal. It ripples out to encompass St. Benedict's community, religious life in general, Christianity, the planet. But for Nancy restlessness, uneasiness, and fear are signs of life. They hint at deep longings lurking just under the surface, waiting to be embodied by someone with courage and a love of plain language.

Sister Arleen Hynes

Sister Arleen Hynes has nine living children, numerous grandchildren, political savvy, an Irish temper that blazes at injustice, and a love of ideas, people, and books. She came to St. Benedict's because of proximity, the Divine Office, and friendship.

In 1941 she and her new husband, Emerson Hynes, settled on ten acres in the woods near St. John's Monastery and University, four miles from St. Benedict's. Emerson had just been hired to teach philosophy and sociology at the University. They moved into a little house the monks helped them build and began their family.

Their goal was to live a simple life made rich by friends, reading, and conversation pursued into the night. They soon had good neighbors—scholars, artists, writers, many of them with connections to the Catholic Worker Movement, some of them pacifists.

Their life was "permeated with the Work of God," Arleen says. They prayed the Divine Office as a family, each child getting an Office book as soon as he or she was able to read. The family was soon large enough to form two choirs.

In 1958 the family moved from this vital place in the woods to Arlington, Virginia, when Emerson became the legislative assistant for Senator Eugene McCarthy, who had been his colleague at St. John's. For thirteen years they worked to translate social concern for groups like migrant workers into political action and law.

Arleen remembers that their kids didn't go to swimming pools or the movies in Arlington because they and their African American friends couldn't go to the same pools or theaters. Even Catholic parishes were segregated. The Hynes family went to church in a black neighborhood, while they worked through the Christian Family Movement to integrate the all-white parish to which they were supposed to belong.

Emerson died in 1971. With three boys still in high school and a mortgage to pay off, Arleen went to work as a librarian at St. Elizabeth's, a federal hospital for the mentally ill. She started reading to the patients, sensing that stories and poetry might be a way to mend damaged minds and spirits. This was the beginning of her work in biblio/poetry therapy. She has set up a training program, published textbooks and articles, and now practices this healing art at St. Benedict's and elsewhere.

In 1980, with her children on their own and the mortgage paid off, Arleen joined St. Benedict's. She came, she says, because she wants to pray the Divine Office with a community as she had for so many years.

Arleen says that family life taught her "to put first things first." When she ponders the *Rule,* she gravitates to practical advice that fits a large family at least as well as it does a community of adults: "Don't grumble." "Practice moderation in all things except justice and compassion." "Those who need more should have it." Another teaching from the *Rule* reinforces an early lesson her foster-mother taught her when, at age five, she and her twin sister ran away from home: "Twins," she said, "you take yourself with you wherever you go. There's no point in running away."

Arleen and Emerson's eighteen-year-old son Michael drowned in the Potomac; she knows about the preciousness and fragility of human life. While contemporary society does not value the wisdom gained from child-rearing, this wisdom is crucial to human survival.

Arleen and women like her who come to St. Benedict's at mid-life or later, with whole lifetimes of experience, provide another clue to what this community might become as it works into the pattern of its life the deep knowledge these women bring with them.

Jana Preble

Jana Preble is not, strictly speaking, a Benedictine. She and her husband Charles, an Anglican priest, are the parents of two grown daughters. Since 1986, they have lived in a farmhouse a few miles from St. Benedict's. On the tree-shaded porch Jana meets the many people who find her a gifted and clear-sighted spiritual guide. In his workshop Charles makes furniture simple and graceful enough to be exhibited in museums and art shows but comfortable and functional as well.

This farmhouse is also the center in the United States for the Order of Agape and Reconciliation, a religious order to which Jana and Charles belong. An ecumenical, contemplative community with its roots in Benedictine monasticism, the order welcomes women and men, married or single, clerics and lay people, who try to live out the Benedictine *Rule* in their daily lives.

Raised in the Methodist church, Jana remembers feeling, even as a child, "a spiritual sensitivity that wasn't nourished." As a young woman she learned to pray the Divine Office from a group of Anglican sisters who ran a summer camp where she worked. Those summers taught her that a life of prayer "is possible no matter what else you do." For Jana, those other things include marriage and motherhood, teaching psychology at St. Cloud State University, counseling, study, and spiritual direction.

Jana got to know St. Benedict's Monastery through Sister Jeremy Hall, who taught theology at Creighton University when Jana was studying there. A few years later she joined the Catholic church; then she and Charles moved to St. Joseph, where they soon became frequent participants at community prayer and Eucharistic celebrations. Jana speaks gratefully of the welcome she and Charles found at St. Benedict's. "We'd be impoverished," she says, "without the support and friendship of this community."

The Benedictine community, in turn, would be impoverished without their angle of vision. The Prebles and other friends help the sisters see the ordinary and extraordinary beauty of their lives. They also offer challenges, asking the sisters to work for economic justice for women, to resist the sexism in the church, not to favor the wealthy over the poor, to help people learn to pray.

The regular presence of women like Jana hints that St. Benedict's boundaries already stretch to include neighbors, colleagues, family members, and former members of this community. These people say simply, without qualification, "I'm Benedictine."

St. Benedict's might also become a place where women can face honestly the differences dividing them from each other and acknowledge the central human search. The members of the Order of Agape and Reconciliation take several vows familiar to Benedictine ears—unconditional love, obedience, nonviolence, simplicity. They also vow joy—an act of sheer daring and hope that sounds utopian until you hear Jana's definition: "At the heart of all that happens, God will meet us."

A line of peace might appear
if we restructured the sentence our lives are making,
revoked its reaffirmation of profit and power,
questioned our needs, allowed
long pauses. . . .

DENISE LEVERTOV[15]

St. Mildred's Abbey

MINSTER, ENGLAND

Minster Abbey, located near the southeast coast of England, was born out of the darkness of World War II. The very stones of its ancient buildings hold a long history of conquest and violence. But this Benedictine community of twelve women brims with a passionate, wide-awake peace.

The first seven sisters to arrive at Minster were literally political refugees, running from Nazi threats to seize St. Walburg Abbey in Eichstätt and expel the sisters. In 1931 and 1935 Abbess Benedicta Von Spiegel set up two monasteries in the United States; and in 1936 she bought the property at Minster as a place of refuge for the Eichstätt sisters should the threat of expulsion become reality. Soon after the seven Eichstätt sisters arrived at Minster, Great Britain entered the war and, because of Minster's strategic location, commandeered the house for the Royal Artillery. The sisters moved to a nearby English men's monastery and spent the war years learning the English language and English customs and farming methods.

After the war, they returned to Minster penniless but eager to stay in England. So, with a few cows, a couple of pigs (with the appropriately British names of Lavender and Primrose), a horse, and the skill of the four Bavarian sisters who had grown up on farms, they turned Minster into a self-supporting working farm. The sisters tell the story of those hard years with zest and humor. The roof of one wing was falling in, and they had no electricity, no running water in the washhouse, and no possibility of financial support from Eichstätt, which had survived the war on CARE packages from two daughter houses in the United States. A neighbor gave them an old Allis Chalmers tractor that none of them knew how to drive. He dictated instructions which one of them wrote down and then read to the designated driver.

It is providence, coincidence, or a great irony of history that the sisters from Eichstätt settled at Minster. Twelve hundred and sixty-six years earlier, in 670, a Saxon noblewoman named Domneva founded St. Mary's Convent near the present Minster. Danish invaders burned this Benedictine monastery to the ground, killing the sisters as well as townspeople and farm workers who had taken refuge there. Saxon and Norman architecture of the buildings at Minster bears silent witness to centuries of violence and intolerance as one conquering tribe after another struggled to rule England. In the succeeding centuries the Benedictine monks from St. Augustine's Abbey in nearby Canterbury built and rebuilt the abbey after the Danes and, two hundred years later, the Normans destroyed it. The Protestant Reformation closed all English monasteries, and in 1538 Minster became royal property, then a private home. Finally, it went on the market just when Mother Benedicta Von Spiegel was looking for a refuge in England.

War has left its mark on the history, the towers, the narrow windows of Minster, through which an archer could aim his bow. The women now living at Minster are not naive enough to think that they left war outside their monastery. For them, as for all of us in this modern age, war shapes and limits imagination and inhabits dreams and language.

The twentieth-century American poet Denise Levertov writes in "Life at War":

> We have breathed the grits of it in
> all our lives,
> our lungs are pocked with it,
> the mucous membranes of our dreams
> coated with it, the imagination
> filmed over with the gray filth of it. . . .[16]

The "it" in these lines is not only war and its residue in our lives. "It" is also human life at war with itself. Against that secret, corrosive presence, the *Rule* of Benedict sets this energetic advice: "Seek after peace and pursue it," or, as another translation says, "Let peace be your quest and aim." No matter how you translate it, Benedictine peace calls for a constant, daily making of peace in a world where *unpeace* reigns.

The making of peace is in some ways the main work of the sisters at Minster, no easy task in such a diverse community. The sisters come from Germany, Romania, Austria, Canada, and England. The prioress, Mother Concordia Scott, identifies herself firmly as Scots-English. In addition to national origin, these twelve sisters differ in gifts, personalities, ages, works, and, most emphatically, opinions. At Minster, peace doesn't come from the blurring or leveling of personalities and views but, rather, from a sharp, beautiful clarity, followed by choices made for the common good. The sisters listen carefully to each other, then disagree vigorously and cheerfully about many subjects, including how they themselves should live Benedictine life.

But they are united in their love for one another and in their desire to make Minster a clear, spacious, windswept place where strangers and surprises are welcome. Questions are not silenced here. Until a couple of years ago some of the sisters who fled from Germany were still alive; surely they remembered and reminded the community of the high cost of silence and unquestioning obedience in Nazi Germany.

This community draws people. Most come willingly—retreatants, musicians and artists, a group of Anglicans who come to pray regularly with the sisters; a few come reluctantly—prisoners on a work-release program who work side by side with the sisters in the fields, gardens, and barns. No one seems to be outside community boundaries. Sister Aelrad Erwin, who extends brisk hospitality and a listening ear to all guests, says, "There's no dividing line between us and other people, at work or at prayer."

Minster is a busy, lively place. But the rhythms of work and prayer, silence and conversation built into Benedictine community life create the long pauses essential to peace. These long pauses allow the clamoring demands for power and possession to quiet down so that the community can hear the needs of the world and answer them gladly.

One of Minster's treasures is a letter written to them by Mother Benedicta Von Spiegel during their hard first year. They had asked the Eichstätt community for money. Even if Eichstätt had had any money to give, they wouldn't have been allowed to send it out of Germany. Mother Benedicta urged them to take to heart the advice from St. Matthew's Gospel: If God cares for the birds of the air and the lilies of the field, surely God would take care of them. Benedicta adds: "It is important that you should have the same spirit as in St. Walburg. . . . Do try to be simple and joyful, and do not give the impression to strangers that you have anxiety or sorrow of any kind. . . . All the people who visit our monastery are deeply impressed with the spirit of simplicity and joy that shines on all our faces. This is what you must aim at. Certainly the Lord will help you. . . ."[17] This letter is the lived charter of the Minster community.

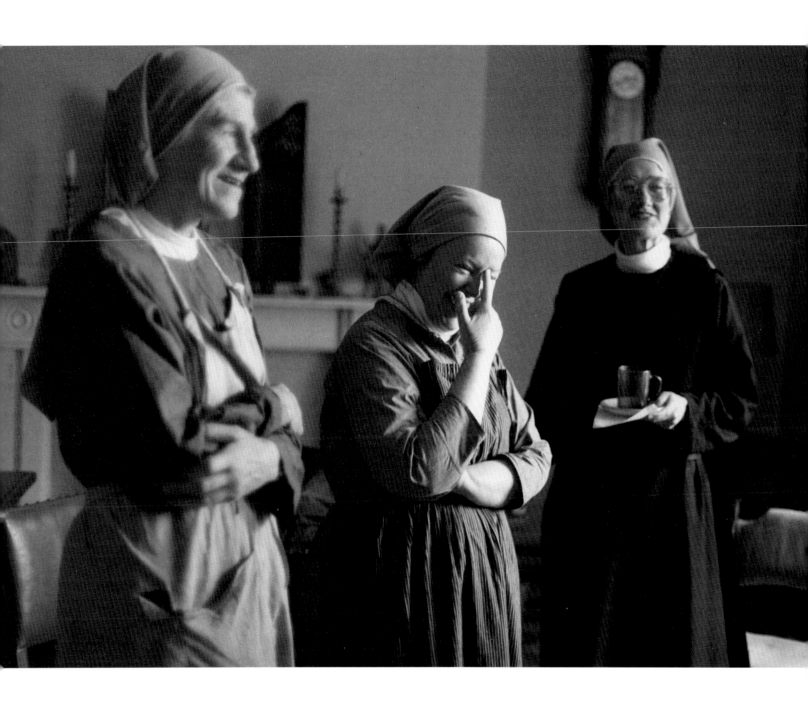

MOTHER CONCORDIA SCOTT

In the seventh century, when Domneva founded the first Benedictine monastery at Minster, the Anglo-Saxons still used the word *frithe-webba* as a synonym for *woman*. It means *peace-weaver*. This beautiful word suggests that peace is something made by hand, and that it is as warm and durable as woven wool or linen. *Webba* also meant spider's web, hinting that peace is woven out of one's own substance, that it connects point to point, that it is sensitive to damage at any point. *Frithe-webba* went out of use hundreds of years ago and now lies buried in the Oxford English Dictionary. But this ancient word perfectly describes Mother Concordia Scott, the current prioress of Minster Abbey. She is quick, talkative, funny, shrewd, an exuberant storyteller who dramatizes everything, including the plight of the Eichstätt sisters before the war. Whether or not it happened just the way she tells it, in her stories Nazi soldiers clatter into the courtyard, march up the abbey steps, and pound on the door. She makes you feel the sisters' fear as she says: "For months they lived on a knife-edge, waiting."

While Mother Concordia's sisters obviously love and support her, they disagree with her as readily as with anyone in the community. She is not one to smooth over differences of opinion. Yet, she seems to know intuitively what makes and what breaks peace on a much deeper level. She understands, for example, that violence to oneself or to others often comes out of the crushing or denying of intelligence and talents. She says, "Here, anyone who has a gift has the time to do it," and "Here, in a small place, every case is different." That generous philosophy might account for the diversity thriving at Minster.

This understanding surely comes in part from her early experience as an artist in a community that needed farmers. Mother Concordia is a sculptor. Her alabaster mother and child stands in Westminster Abbey and her bronze Our Lady of Fifth Avenue in the Anglican Church of St. Thomas in New York City. After serving in the British army as a radar operator, she joined Minster Abbey in 1953. She had some training in art, but the struggling community needed her to take her turn driving the Allis Chalmers tractor and doing dozens of other practical tasks. In the 1960s Mother Walburga Von Walburg-Zeil, the prioress, understood that both Concordia and the community needed art, not just as relics from the past but as part of their daily life. Mother Walburga gave her a studio with windows and daily time to practice her sculpture.

"Being in a monastery and being an artist is a perfect combination," Mother Concordia says. Hearing about her past and present life, other artists might not agree. Because this is a small community, everyone has several jobs. You might find Concordia in her studio pouring a bronze casting. But you'll be just as likely to spy her hurrying down the street of Minster, satchel in hand, bent upon some financial errand as community treasurer, or taking her turn greeting guests at the front door, or kneeling in prayer. She says, "I try not to put the artist first."

Mother Concordia's work as an artist and the pieces she creates don't stand on a pedestal in this community. They are as central to the life of the monastery as prayer and tasty food, but they are not exalted above the other work that goes on there. Her work seems to be roughly on a par with raising sheep, writing history, caring for the old sisters, greeting and feeding guests. At Minster, all work done well, with craft and love, is art; art done well, with full concentation of all one's human energies, is work. Much better than being separate and exalted, her work and her works are integral to the life of the community, where the quiet strength of her Madonna and Child calls to mind the strong, daring women who have lived at Minster for centuries.

Like the rest of the sisters at Minster, Mother Concordia understands the subtle connection between peace and plenty. Needing, wanting, having too much disrupts the common good, both inside and outside the monastery. Everything about their lives is simple, unadorned. With no apologies, they and their guests sit down to very simple meals. Mother Concordia jokes about their frugality: "I'm a Scot—I watch our pennies." No doubt she does. But that frugality makes generosity possible. Mother Concordia never talks about it, but her sisters know that money flows freely through her hands to hands reaching out in need. She doesn't make careful year-end calculations, and then give what the community can easily afford, because those sitting around the common table of the world can't wait till year's end to be fed. Rather, she often gives money the community doesn't have, trusting that the God of sparrows and lilies will make up the difference.

SISTER JOHN FLORESCU

Sister John Florescu came to Minster from Romania, via Canada and the United States. She is at home in her old work clothes, looking bedraggled and ill at ease in the Benedictine habit she wears for meals and prayer. Sister John has what she calls "a charism for chickens and ducks." That description hints at her ironical wit, as she brings the lofty notion of charism into the farmyard with its ripe sounds and smells. Those birds are a point of contention between her and Sister Ancilla, the chief farmer: Sister John likes her roosters too much to serve them to fussy retreatants who don't like mutton. Her thoughts and her conversation range widely from chickens, to the economic necessities that guide communal decisions, to Zen. "Zen Buddhists," she says, "take in suffering and turn it into something else, so that not even suffering is wasted."

Sister Ancilla Dent

Before she came to Minster, Sister Ancilla Dent was a lawyer. Now this plain-spoken Englishwoman runs the Minster farm, raising sheep and angora goats. She says the same thing about farming that Mother Concordia says about art—farming and monasticism make a good combination. Or, as she puts it in her unflowery way, "Being with nature fits with the monastic thing." In fact, she recently edited a collection of Pope John Paul II's writings on ecology. Ancilla is the first to puncture any utopian ideas about Minster. She says that the members hold conflicting ideas about the direction the community ought to take, each of them supporting a traditional Benedictine value: they should pray more, spend more time together, extend greater hospitality to guests, work more in gardens and studios. With her feet firmly planted in this community, Ancilla points out that the balanced life Benedictines are known for is often precarious, needing conversation, compromise, and daily conversion.

The body *characterizes* everything it touches. What it makes it traces over with the marks of its pulses and breathings, its excitements, hesitations, flaws, and mistakes. On its good work, it leaves the marks of skill, care, and love persisting through hesitations, flaws, and mistakes. And to those of us who love and honor the life of the body in this world, these marks are precious things, necessities of life.

WENDELL BERRY[18]

Abbey of St. Walburga

BOULDER, COLORADO

It's evening at St. Walburga's Abbey near Boulder, Colorado. Summertime. The uncut alfalfa is fragrant and purple, and the Rocky Mountains to the west are many shades of gray, edged in pale yellow. An hour earlier, a thunder and hailstorm sent the cattle galloping towards home, bellowing in fear, but now the cows and their calves graze quietly as if nothing had happened. In the thin, clear air, the leaves of a big old cottonwood rustle, while the nearby freeway sends up its unending, monotonous hum.

Everything here—the fields, the Abbey, the guest houses—speaks of patience, that most un-American of qualities. Nothing happens quickly here. You will find no sixty-minute management, no instant intimacy, no quick fixes, forced growth, harvesting of unripened fruits.

The first place to look for the source of this patience is the land itself, the hundred and sixty acres several generations of Benedictine women have coaxed into green bounty. Three sisters came to Boulder from Eichstätt in 1935; four more arrived in 1937. As at Minster, these women were political refugees, and the monastery was to be a safe haven in case the Nazis turned the Eichstätt sisters out of their home. Even though a succession of farmers hadn't been able to get anything to grow on this high plain, the sisters didn't give up on their unyielding piece of land. Instead, they learned how to irrigate from a neighboring farmer, bought pants and high boots on credit from a friendly storekeeper, and went to work. By the time World War II had impoverished the community in Eichstätt, they were able to support themselves as well as send CARE packages of food and medicine to Germany.

The dry, rocky land now yields enough feed for a herd of fifty dairy cows, which the sisters plan to increase to seventy cow-calf pairs. The monastery itself has grown from a leaky-roofed farmhouse, lacking windows and indoor plumbing, to a new motherhouse and accommodations for as many as forty-five guests and retreatants.

Another source of the patience that fills this community is a series of clear choices the sisters have made during their sixty-two years in the United States. While they agree that Benedictine life is organic, changing to fit different times, places, and cultures, they have held steadfastly to what they consider essential values and practices, often with considerable difficulty. The first seven sisters quickly learned to speak English, exchanging supper for daily lessons from the parish priest. They learned to read it by studying obituaries, figuring that all obituaries say pretty much the same thing. More recently, they did their own English translation of the Divine Office. Even though many of the sisters are native-born Germans, the whole community speaks English at meals. The prioress, Mother Maria-Thomas Beil, says, "We are an American community."

But in many important ways the community is not typical of the United States or, perhaps, of the modern world. From the beginning, Colorado priests and bishops pressured the sisters to "do something useful," like teach or run a hospital. In their opinion a community occupied only with prayer, solitude, silence, and farm work was societal deadwood. To make matters worse, in the early years the community was divided between those who wanted to pray more and those who wanted to get on with the farm work. In spite of internal and external pressures, the community now comes together six times a day to pray and to allow silence to speak.

Unlike many American Benedictines, these women wear traditional garb, with a few common-sense modifications (jeans, work shirts, and sneakers for operating tractors and balers.) Something more substantial than nostalgia or the romance of wearing a medieval costume led to this community decision. Religious dress is called a *habit,* and the wisdom of the language asserts that in putting on this habit the women also put on habits of thought and action that have worn well for hundreds of years. Habits of equality and commitment to one another "until death," as the *Rule* of Benedict says, make these women sisters.

The *Rule* also urges Benedictines to "support with the greatest patience one another's weaknesses of body or behavior." These women can afford to be patient with themselves and each other because they have the time and every good reason to work out differences and dissension.

Rather than the familiar gulf between generations, old and young live and work intimately together. On the farm, for instance, the young sisters learn from the pioneers when the alfalfa is ready to cut or how to pull a calf from a cow in distress. A younger sister says, "It's a joy that we have the old sisters. There's a holiness about them. You can see all those years of prayer. And at seventy or eighty, they're still working to change."

Faithfulness to the daily round of prayer, work, and celebration and contact with the patient land through cycles of drought and rain as the seasons roll in over the mountains yield a remarkable clarity and steadfastness of purpose. Sister Hildegard Dubnick, who joined the community a few years ago, says she came because the sisters are who they say they are. She was studying linguistic anthropology at the University of Chicago. Now she operates the computer, puts out a newsletter, and helps with yardwork and haying. In the silence, she says, boredom, restlessness, and the deceptive allure of endless choice have fallen away. Though she might question a community decision or the way a job is being done, she never wonders, "Why bother? Why are we doing these things at all—praying, working, trying to live gracefully with each other?"

The life at St. Walburga's Abbey continues to evolve. Mother Maria-Thomas encourages art and music; and as more college-educated women join the community, scholarship and study no doubt will become more important. But these women probably will continue to resist the cycle of escalating consumption and busyness eroding natural and human life. Sister Mary Michael says simply, "I never go to prayer by myself. The world is so busy people don't have time to be in chapel. I sit in for them and represent them. My work is to bring them before God and say, 'Here are your people.'"

SISTER ANGELA WÜRZBURGER

SISTER MARY MICHAEL NEWE

Age, language, culture, and history divide these two farm women. Sister Mary Michael is in her thirties, Sister Angela in her eighties. Mary Michael grew up in Whittier, California, in the 1960s, a few minutes by freeway from Los Angeles. Angela grew up on a big German farm within walking distance of St. Walburg Abbey in Eichstätt. She joined the abbey after World War I, when Germany, or rather the German middle class, was still paying the huge war reparations decreed by the Treaty of Versailles. She remembers coming home for visits and finding notes attached to a cow or her bed: "To be sold for taxes." At that time, she says, her people were a hundred percent for Hitler because he promised to keep German money at home.

What unites Mary Michael and Angela goes much deeper than these differences in age and origin. While they are worlds away from their California and Germany childhoods, both of them scorn the idea that they are quaint, picturesque, or unusual. They matter-of-factly do what farm women around the world have always done—work hard with animals and the land to maintain life. Both of them know what it's like to be in the barn at four every morning, in all kinds of weather, milking cows and feeding chickens. They know what it's like to watch the summer sky anxiously, wondering if the rain will hold off so they can bring in the alfalfa. Both are self-sufficient and self-confident. Angela, who was the first in the community to don pants and boots and crawl down into irrigation ditches, says with quiet pride, "I'm a good irrigator." City-bred Mary Michael, who has managed the farm for the past ten years, keeps the machinery running; with the same offhand pride she says, "I'm mechanical. I can fix things."

Patience, passion, and *compassion* all come from the same ancient root, a word meaning *to suffer, to feel deeply, to endure, to stick it out to the end.* Both Mary Michael and Angela are passionate about life, their passion expressing itself in action rather than in words. Mary Michael is attentive to the effects their farm practices have on the environment. Within the next few years, she intends to replace their acres of alfalfa with grass hay, because alfalfa gets weevils, which have to be sprayed with pesticide if you want a crop. "We have no right to do that," Mary Michael says. She knows her cows by personality and name—Annie-Get-Your-Gun, the star of the herd, Dove, the gentle one, and Mercy, who gives the most milk. On summer evenings after work and prayers are finished, she strides down the pasture trail with Amber (the Great Dane pup) running circles around her, both of them obviously in love with the sunset and the smell of rain and freshly cut hay.

Sister Angela has endured many kinds of suffering—the poverty and backbreaking work of the thirties, Hitler's threat to her family, community, and homeland, a bout with cancer, changes within her Benedictine community. Suffering could have broken or embittered her. Instead, it weathered and toughened her like stone worn smooth or the great exposed roots of the cottonwood tree in the pasture. It has left her wise and cheerful, ready to laugh or tell a good story.

Yet, Angela knows the worst that human beings can do to each other. Not long after she came to Boulder, news of Hitler's death camps began to arrive, and she knew that her Catholic family was in danger. More than fifty years later she remembers that fear. She and the other sisters at Boulder had prepared to become United States citizens. On the day of the test the examiner asked Sister Angela the names of her cows. In her newly acquired English she rattled off the names of German rivers and towns. Then he asked about the bull. His name was Hitler, she told him, and her mean-tempered ganders were Hitler and Mussolini. The examiner approved of her sentiments. But Angela says fiercely, "I thought to myself, if Hitler knew I named my bull after him, my family would end up in Dachau."

Angela relishes the stories about their early hard days, when the sisters worked together to dig a basement under the old farmhouse. They had a shovel and pickaxe—and their aprons to carry out the dirt and rock. Angela noticed an unused wheelbarrow in the parish cemetery. She "borrowed" it, on the good logic that they needed it and no one was using it just then. She doesn't think they ever returned it. On rainy nights they went to bed in their leaky house with umbrellas over their beds, and they swished the snow off the outhouse seat with those useful aprons.

When you ask Angela how they did it, she shrugs and smiles and answers as many courageous women do, "I don't know. We just did it."

At age eighty, she supposedly retired. "I've worked enough," she says. But if you want to find her, look outside, where she's likely to be sweeping out the granary or feeding the chickens or the peacocks who belong to the neighbors but come to the abbey to eat. Like any good gardener, Angela never passes by a geranium wilting in the Colorado heat without giving it a cupful of water.

Sister Mary Michael says that she brings her work to prayer. For her, and especially for Sister Angela, the divisions between work and prayer have disappeared into a single-hearted simplicity. Having walked "all the hard and rugged ways by which the journey to God is made," as the *Rule* says, they now "run the way of God's commandments with the inexpressible sweetness of love."

Pilgrim:
when your ship,
long moored in harbour,
gives you the illusion
of being a house;
when your ship
begins to put down roots
in the stagnant waters of the
quay:
put out to sea!
Save your boat's journeying soul
cost what it may.

DOM HELDER CÂMARA[19]

Recife, Pernambuco

BRAZIL

It is early morning in Jordão, or Jordan, a section of Recife in the poverty-stricken northeastern corner of Brazil. The air is already hot. In the distance the sea glistens. The first sound is the breeze rustling in dry corn plants. The second is the music, amplified and distorted, that blares from the plaza every day from dawn until dark. The day opens with the Peace Prayer of St. Francis and closes with the Ave Maria. During all the hours in between, fifties rock and roll, much of it imported from the United States, cancels silence.

Soon after the music starts, there is the sound of hands clapping outside the home of three Benedictine sisters, as visitors politely announce their presence. Every day they come, in a long procession, to ask the sisters for a kilo of beans, a kilo of rice, dried milk for the children, *farinha* to fill the empty spaces.

Sometimes the children themselves come. This morning, the first person to appear is a small boy named Messias, along with his scrawny puppy and his baby cousin with her crooked foot. In return for food, he smiles patiently and answers the questions of these powerful women from the United States.

Almost twenty-five years ago, Sister Madonna Kuebelbeck came to Recife from St. Benedict's Monastery in St. Joseph, Minnesota. Since then, five other sisters have followed, staying for varying lengths of time. Though they are competent teachers, nurses, musicians, or administrators, they didn't come to set up schools or clinics. The reason each woman came to Recife is both complex—entangled with personal experiences and chance—and simple; each of them heard and answered the urging of the gospels and the *Rule* of St. Benedict to look for Christ in the poor. The images of oppression and poverty filtering into their lives made each of them trade the safe harbor of life in Minnesota for the uncertainty and danger of life in Recife.

The sisters' life in Jordão is almost as far as it is possible to be from central Minnesota. They live in a simple four-bedroom house made of cinder blocks. Out back is the *lavandaria,* or laundry, where the sisters wash their clothes by hand; in front is a little terrace. They share their uncertain supply of water with a few corn plants, a hibiscus or two, and a coconut palm. The house often rings with laughter, rowdy card games, and the vigorous give and take of community life. Sometimes, in troubled conversations, the sisters marvel at the heartbreaking beauty and cruelty of this country and the sturdy spirit of the people.

The sisters' home is just on the edge of an "invasion," a squatters' settlement that grew up almost overnight when the government opened the area to displaced families. Ten years ago it was empty land; now more than twenty thousand people live in tiny wood or brick houses crowded together on the red hillsides. Most of the people get water from communal spigots and electricity by tapping illegally into the high lines. Records in Brasilia, the capital, claim that money has been appropriated and spent to pave the streets of Jordão. In reality, most of them are dirt, dusty in the dry season, treacherous red rivers of mud in the rainy season, always rutted and potholed.

This *favela,* or slum, gets its name from the Jordão River flowing through it. Since the *favela* enjoys almost no sanitary facilities, the stream collects raw sewage from the people living near it and gives back parasites and disease to the children playing along its banks. The children sail scraps of wood, small boats with no access to the sea.

The Benedictine sisters often ask themselves how they should live here. As white women from the United States, every decision or action sends potent messages to the people with whom they live and work.

Should they, for instance, hire Brazilian women to cook and keep house for them? That help would free the sisters from the seemingly endless chores required for maintaining life and health with few technological aids, and would support a couple of fatherless households. But the sisters wonder how they can claim to be walking down those rutted roads alongside the people of Jordão when those people are in the kitchen cooking their meals or out in the *lavandaria* scrubbing their clothes.

The sisters spend the first hour of every day sitting together in silent prayer, and then praying the Divine Office. They've asked themselves whether they should take time to eat and celebrate as a community, spend days on the beach, or even pray in a place where needs and problems seem to demand constant attention. During prayer, they often have to ignore the insistent clapping of hands outside their door.

But this quiet hour, before the noise and busyness of the day begin, centers them and at the same time helps them "burst the thick wall of self," as writer Tillie Olsen describes one essential human task.[20] For them, as for all Benedictines, the psalms remind them daily that their lives are not the only lives that matter. They faithfully pray psalms of joy when they are feeling anything but joyful, and psalms of exile, loneliness, and oppression even when they are feeling at home, loved, and useful.

The hardest puzzle of all is what work women from the United States can or should do in Recife. Convinced that they are not messiahs, these educated, efficient, energetic women have learned the hard lesson of patience: they wait until the people and their situation ask something of them.

Those *somethings* are usually simple and their effects apparently fleeting. The sisters might take a sick child to the clinic, help plan a liturgical celebration, or encourage the vital young women who teach Bible school. Or they might simply help celebrate the seventy-fifth birthday of Maria Jose, as Jeanie (Sister Jeanne Schwartz) did one day, crossing the Jordão River on a perilous wooden bridge, cake in hand, gathering in her wake a procession of women and children.

The sisters often wonder what ripples their presence makes in the vast living sea surrounding them. Their real poverty is not the small deprivations of their lives but seeing need all around them and not being able to alleviate it.

SISTER ELLEN COTONE—ELENA

In Recife, it is impossible to forget that people have bodies. The flamboyant beauty of ocean, sky, and tropical flowers charm the senses, while incessant noise and the unrelenting smells caused by poverty and poor sanitation assault them. Sickness and death are daily concerns. Once when she had both fleas and intestinal parasites, Sister Ellen Cotone—Elena—wrote to her brother that she "felt like the family dog."

Elena came to Recife at age sixty, after a lifetime as a musician, teacher, and liturgist. After five years she was still struggling to learn Portuguese. That struggle has taught her what it means to be submerged in a "culture of silence." The revolutionary Brazilian educator, Paulo Freire, uses that phrase to describe the vast culture of the oppressed, who are not allowed to define themselves and who cannot make language work for them, even to get their simplest needs met.[21] In spite of the constant barrage of noise, Jordão is a culture of silence, and Elena is a part of it. Neither hers nor the people's words can assure a steady supply of safe water, regular garbage pick-up, education for the children, or jobs that pay a living wage.

Yet Elena considers herself very lucky to be in Recife, and she subverts the silence by making music with people like herself who hear melodies and carry rhythms in their bodies. She plays an electronic keyboard in church and gives music lessons. Some evenings musicians gather in the sisters' living room and music spills out of the little house—Bach toccatas, Brazilian pop tunes, protest songs never heard in the plaza.

Elena also subverts silence by carrying the Eucharist, Christ's eloquent body, to people too old or sick to come to church. She prays with the people, then stays for coffee and conversation made up of smiles, gestures, a few Portuguese phrases, a warm hug.

Elena says, "God has a passion for every one of us, and I'm lucky enough that God has this passion for me." With or without words, she wants to convince the people of Jordão of God's and her love for them.

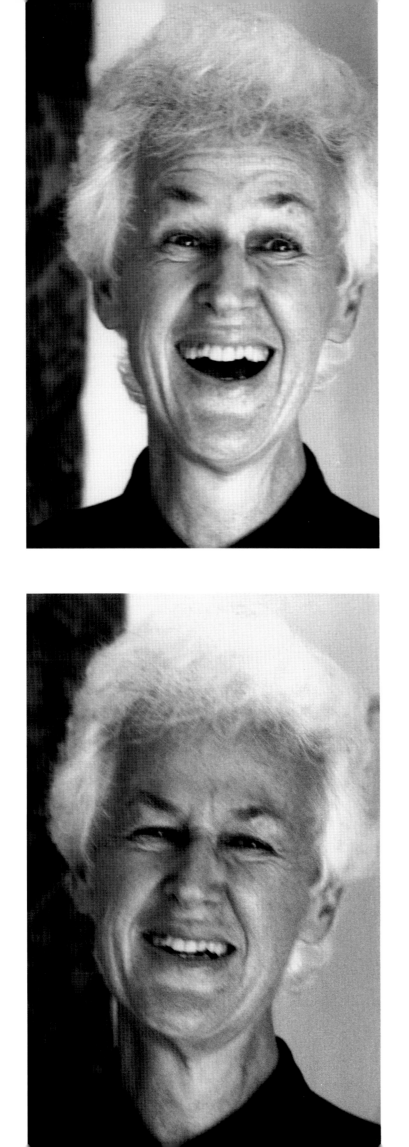

SISTER KERRY O'REILLY—KÁTIA

Sister Kerry O'Reilly, called Kátia by the people of Jordão, is a natural leader—decisive, warm, quick to laugh or argue, and at her best when a crisis erupts. Those qualities have been blessing and curse during her eleven years in Brazil. Because of colonialism, periods of dictatorial rule, and many other sorts of oppression, "Brazilians are almost paralyzed by anyone who has even a hint of authority or know-how," Kátia says. She came to the parish of São João Batista in 1983; four years later the parish priest left, and no one came to replace him. "They tried their darndest to make me the priest!" she says. Because she wanted the people to realize their own authority, she refused: "I used all my energy in *not* doing anything. There we were, all of us, doing nothing together." (Eventually, Kátia and three women of the parish became the administrators.)

During Kátia's years in Brazil, an elected government replaced the military dictatorship, but with the minimum salary at forty-two dollars a month and annual inflation sometimes as high as 1800 percent, the plight of the working people has not improved. Divisions within the Catholic church deepened, as liberation theology and base communities fell under suspicion.

Through these discouraging years Kátia tried to imagine alternatives to existing conditions and to help the people of Jordão do the same. Though she speaks fluent Portuguese, she realizes that her ability to "hear people into speech" (to use theologian Nelle Morton's phrase) is more important than her words.[22] "I can't solve the people's problems," she says. "All I can give is time, an ear. I try to feel what a person or group is feeling and help them move out of confusion into growth." She respects the people's self-definitions, their names for themselves: "They call themselves *gente,* the people, not *pobre,* the poor, or *pequenos,* the little ones."

Kátia came to Brazil, she says, partly because the Benedictine life she was living in Minnesota seemed closed in on itself. But living in Recife has not silenced her questions. She says, "I don't think we Benedictines live radically or simply. We've transported many U.S. standards to Jordão." That's hard for most visitors from the United States to believe. The sisters sleep under mosquito nets, are regularly dosed for intestinal parasites, and tell stories—hilarious only in retrospect—of falling into open sewers and watching helplessly as a whole hillside washed into and through their house. But Kátia reminds herself that St. Benedict's monastery and many friends in the states provide reliable financial support that buys health care, a house, travel, entertainment, and safe water; this support buys nutritious food for themselves and the growing crowd of people who come to their door.

Kátia says, "It's the divisions that hurt me so much." She means those between rich and poor in Brazil, between church factions, between conventional notions of God and the Kingdom and the reality she sees every day in Jordão, between her desire to trust fully in God and her need to change social structures. Against all evidence, she repeats the words of Dom Helder Câmara, the charismatic former archbishop of Recife-Olinda: "Misery will not have the last word."

SISTER MARY SCHUMER—MARIANA

Every week Mariana—Sister Mary Schumer—goes to the Lar do Nenê, an orphanage in downtown Recife, where she spends a few hours taking care of babies and toddlers. These children have food, clothes, and a group of loving volunteers who cuddle and play with them and call them by name—Tadeo, Nancy, Jamile, Igor. Every now and then a child is adopted by a Brazilian or foreign family. Mariana knows these children are among the lucky ones.

In northeastern Brazil, both in the cites and on the great sugar cane plantations, 85 percent of the children are malnourished; every hour, six die of preventable diseases. Millions are homeless, but life is perilous even for those with homes. When asked what they want for their children, many parents answer, "That they'll grow up" or "That they won't sink from poverty into misery." (*Poverty* means parents can feed and shelter their children; *misery* means they can't.)

But whether living in poverty or misery, many children have no childhood. On beaches lined by shopping malls and luxury hotels, skinny boys spend their days selling frozen treats and pigeon eggs to tourists and middle-class Brazilians. If the sales go well, they might bring forty-five cents home to their mothers. Instead of playing or going to school, they walk the beaches from seven in the morning until four in the afternoon, calling their wares—"Picolé-olé!" Homeless children beg leftovers from patrons at sidewalk cafes, scooping scraps into plastic bags and taking them around the corner to share with their buddies.

Mariana's heart is with these children and their mothers and grandmothers, whom she often visits in their homes, where three or four generations live together. Her quiet eyes invite the women to tell her their stories. From these stories, she has learned both the similarities between her life and theirs and the vast, troubling differences.

Mariana has learned, for example, about the women of Jussaral, a village north of Recife. Three hundred years ago European colonizers began to strip the virgin timber from the hills. Now, every square foot is planted in sugar cane, an extremely lucrative crop for the plantation owners. Twenty-five years ago most of the owners were Brazilian, and the profits stayed in the country; now multinational corporations own half the land. The workers—men, women, and older children—cut cane from four until ten in the morning and load it on trucks in the afternoon to be taken to the refinery. A strong young man can make $4.50 a day.

The wives of the cane workers of Jussaral are denied basic human rights both by their husbands and by the plantation owners. Called together by another group of North American sisters, they gather in small groups to read Bible stories and to talk, naming a favorite flower, a favorite color. Plantation overseers break up these gatherings, realizing that women with voices and preferences are dangerous.

Yet, living in Jussaral are women like Dona Rosa, from whom Mariana gains strength and wisdom. Dona Rosa seems to do everything from scrubbing clothes in the stream to caring for her grandchildren to midwifery with the same cheerful, hopeful competence.

While Mariana is the first to point out the differences between her life and the lives of women like Dona Rosa, her thirteen years in Brazil have transformed her, creating a secet kinship. She talks of the loneliness of life in Recife, of missing family, friends, her Benedictine community in Minnesota, her native language and culture. But these difficulties have taught her a crucial lesson that binds her to the women of Jordão and Jussaral. She says quietly, "Even if we lose everything, nothing and nobody can take away God's love."

Afterword

We end this book as we began with Dona Rosa and our central question: What do Benedictine women have in common with each other and with the world's women? What hungers unite and divide us? Our answers to those questions are tentative and partial. Benedictine communities grow organically, taking their shape and color from inner and outer circumstances. The gifts of each member, the needs of the society, the steady guidance of the *Rule*, and fifteen hundred years of tradition come together in a creative push and pull, making every Benedictine monastery autonomous and unlike every other one. There are also interesting likenesses. History shows that Benedictine monasteries often have been places where women learned, created, and trusted their intuitions of God and of human life.

But these monasteries have never been serene oases. It would be more accurate to say that Benedictines, like women in every walk of life, every social class, and every age, take what life gives them—the oppression and freedom, the poverty and riches, the containment and scope—and try to make something useful and beautiful. And the women we talked with know that just as the arms of a family are too fragile to protect children in a world not safe for children, so the arms of a community provide women with only illusory shelter in a world where any woman is in danger.

Benedictines have no monopoly on the hungers we've named in this book—for peace; for connections with God, each other, the earth, their deepest selves; for compassion given and received; for satisfying, creative, *needed* work that doesn't overwhelm the rest of life; for continuity and sustaining prayer; for a centered life that frees us to dance on the very edge of possibility.

St. Benedict's counsel does not try to dull these hungers or wish them away; rather it makes them sharp, clear, even painful, so that they lead to an energetic, hopeful reaching out: "Listen and incline the ear of your heart." "Let all things be common to all." "Take care of the sick, the old, children, the poor, pilgrims." "Help those in trouble." "Seek God's justice and never despair of God's mercy." These hungers, once we have let ourselves feel them, make us forever dissatisfied with grayness and passivity. As Audre Lorde says, they teach us "not to settle for the convenient, the shoddy, the conventionally expected, nor the merely safe."[23]

We have told the stories of these six Benedictine communities and of a few of the women who belong to each of them, knowing that these sketches do not begin to do justice to the vitality and richness we found. Words and photographs cannot freeze life, and individuals and communities keep moving on. In the few years since we completed our interviews, new stories have sprung up, stories of death and new life. Sisters from every monastery have died, and every monastery has welcomed new members. In tune with the traditional Benedictine commitment to autonomy, Minster Abbey has become independent. Needing more space and eager to get away from the noise of the freeway, St. Walburga's is preparing to move from their original site near Boulder to a new piece of land near the Wyoming border. Kátia—Sister Kerry O'Reilly—is studying at the Catholic Theological Union in Chicago in preparation for her return to Recife. Believing that "making great beauty in the inner city could change the world," Mount St. Benedict's Monastery recently opened the Inner-City Neighborhood Art House in Erie. St. Benedict's Monastery marked the one hundred fortieth anniversary of their arrival in Minnesota by making plans for a combination heritage center, art gallery, and work spaces for community and visiting artists.

We hope this book is an open invitation to all our readers to tell their own stories. The generous white spaces surrounding pictures and words suggest the book's themes—silence, mystery, hunger. The spaces also reverberate with all the stories that remain to be told about these and other monastic communities and about women around the world whose lives are just beginning to emerge from silence.

The words, too, are an invitation—to agreement, questions, and challenges, the more honest and direct, the better. It is easy to anticipate some of them because they are our questions too: In what ways have Benedictine women cooperated in their own oppression and that of other women? Are we silent when we ought to speak? Can women who live in comfort recognize their own silenced, hungry selves in the women of Jussaral? Dare we claim kinship? Can Benedictine women play a part in the emergence of women leaders in Christian and other religious traditions?

Finally, the photographs gather around themselves a circle of attentive watchers and invite a response that goes beyond words. We hope that warm eyes, curved backs, and work-toughened hands will reach across the gulfs created by circumstance, inviting readers to try on lives different from their own.

Notes

1. Maya Angelou, from "Alone," *The Complete Collected Poems of Maya Angelou* (New York: Random House, 1994), p. 74.

2. Audre Lorde, "The Master's Tools Will Never Dismantle the Master's House," in *This Bridge Called My Back: Writings by Radical Women of Color*, ed. Cherríe Moraga and Gloria Anzaldúa (Watertown, Mass.: Persephone, 1981), pp. 98-99.

3. Adrienne Rich, "Resisting Amnesia: History and Personal Life," *Ms.*, March 1987, p. 67.

4. Michael Dennis Browne, from "Talk to me, Baby," *The Sun Fetcher* (Pittsburgh: Carnegie-Mellon Univ. Press, 1978), p. 83.

5. Annie Dillard, *Pilgrim at Tinker Creek* (New York: Harper's Magazine Press, 1974), p. 242.

6. All subsequent quotations from the *Rule* are taken from *The Rule of Benedict in English*, ed. Timothy Fry, O.S.B. (Collegeville, Minn.: Liturgical Press, 1982) or *St. Benedict's Rule for Monasteries*, trans. Leonard J. Doyle (Collegeville, Minn.: Liturgical Press, 1948).

7. Mary Lou Kownacki, O.S.B., *Peace Is Our Calling: Contemporary Monasticism and the Peace Movement* (Erie, Pa.: Benet Press, 1981), p. 179.

8. "Monastic Life Today," *The Mount* 6, no. 1 (1993): 10-11.

9. Mary Lou Kownacki, O.S.B., "God Is Already Here: The Spiritual Journey," *The Mount* 6, no. 1 (1993): 5.

10. Julian of Norwich, *Julian of Norwich: Showings*, trans. and ed. Eric Colledge and James Walsh (New York: Paulist Press, 1978), p. 284.

11. Historical material on St. Benedict's Monastery is taken from Grace McDonald, O.S.B., *With Lamps Burning* (St. Paul, Minn.: North Central Publishing Co. for St. Benedict's Convent, St. Joseph, Minn., 1957), Ephrem Hollermann, O.S.B., *The Shaping of a Tradition: American Benedictine Women 1852-1881* (St. Joseph, Minn.: Sisters of the Order of St. Benedict, 1994), and the St. Benedict's Monastery archives.

12. Katherine Kraft, O.S.B., "Why Monastic Life in the Late Twentieth Century: Testimonies of Perception," *American Benedictine Review*, Sept. 1995, p. 343.

13. Tillie Olsen, "I Stand Here Ironing," *Tell Me a Riddle* (New York: Laurel-Dell, 1981), pp. 9, 17.

14. Julian of Norwich, p. 153.

15. Denise Levertov, from "Making Peace," *Breathing the Water* (New York: New Directions, 1987), p. 40.

16. Denise Levertov, from "Life at War," *The Sorrow Dance* (New York: New Directions, 1966), p. 79.

17. Mother Concordia Scott, O.S.B., *A Brief History of Minster Abbey: 1937–1987* (Ramsgate, Kent: Minster Abbey, 1987), n.p.

18. Wendell Berry, "Feminism, the Body, and the Machine," *What Are People For?* (San Francisco: North Point Press, 1990), p. 194.

19. Dom Helder Câmara, *A Thousand Reasons for Living*, ed. José de Broucker, trans. Alan Neame (Philadelphia: Fortress Press, 1981), p. 40.

20. Tillie Olsen, quoted by Erika Duncan, "Tillie Olsen," in *Unless Soul Clap Its Hands: Portraits and Passages* (New York: Schocken Books, 1984), p. 39.

21. Paulo Freire, *Pedagogy of the Oppressed*, trans. Myra Bergman Ramos (New York: Continuum, 1992), pp. 13-14.

22. Nelle Morton, *The Journey Is Home* (Boston: Beacon Press, 1985), p. 99.

23. Audre Lorde, *Uses of the Erotic: The Erotic as Power* (Trumansburg, N.Y.: Out and Out Books, 1978), n.p.

List of Photographs

The duotone photographs in *Born of Common Hungers* were prepared by Mossberg & Company, Inc., South Bend, Indiana, and Juanita Dix, South Bend, Indiana, and were printed by World Wide Graphics, Inc., Bloomington, Indiana on 100 # White Quintessence Dull Enamel paper.

The book was designed by Will H. Powers, after the original layout of Annette Brophy and Mara Faulkner, and composed at Stanton Publication Services, Inc., St. Paul, Minnesota.

Text was set in ITC Legacy, designed by Ron Arnholm. Legacy reinterprets Renaissance masterpieces for digital composition. The roman is based on a type cut in Venice by Nicolas Jenson (1469). The model for the italic was cut in Paris by Claude Garamond (1539). The display type is Albertus, designed by Berthold Wolpe (1932).